Witchy

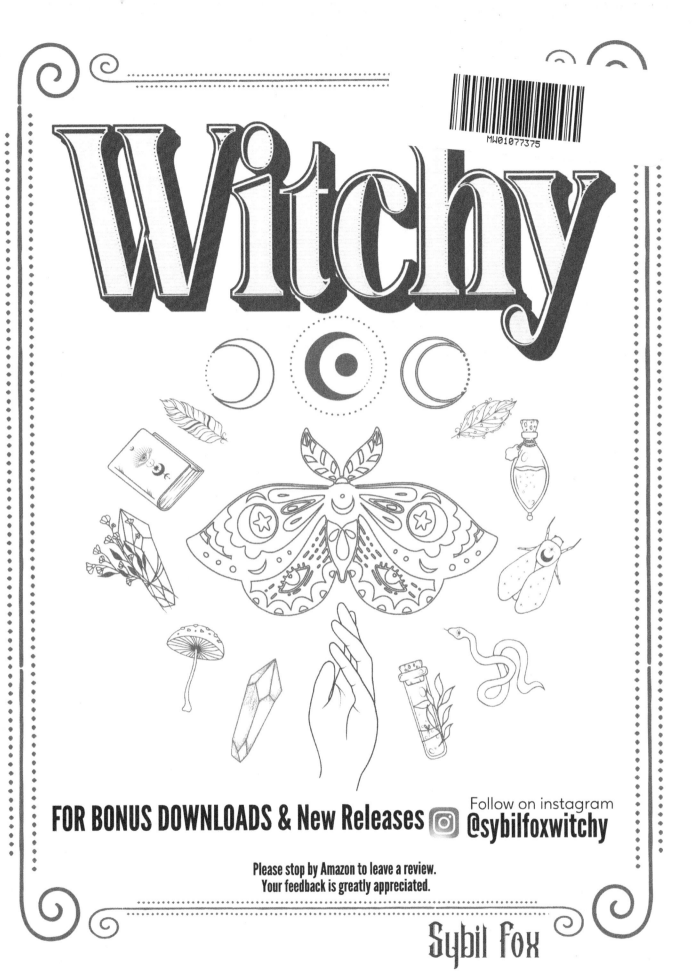

FOR BONUS DOWNLOADS & New Releases 📷 Follow on instagram
@sybilfoxwitchy

Sybil Fox

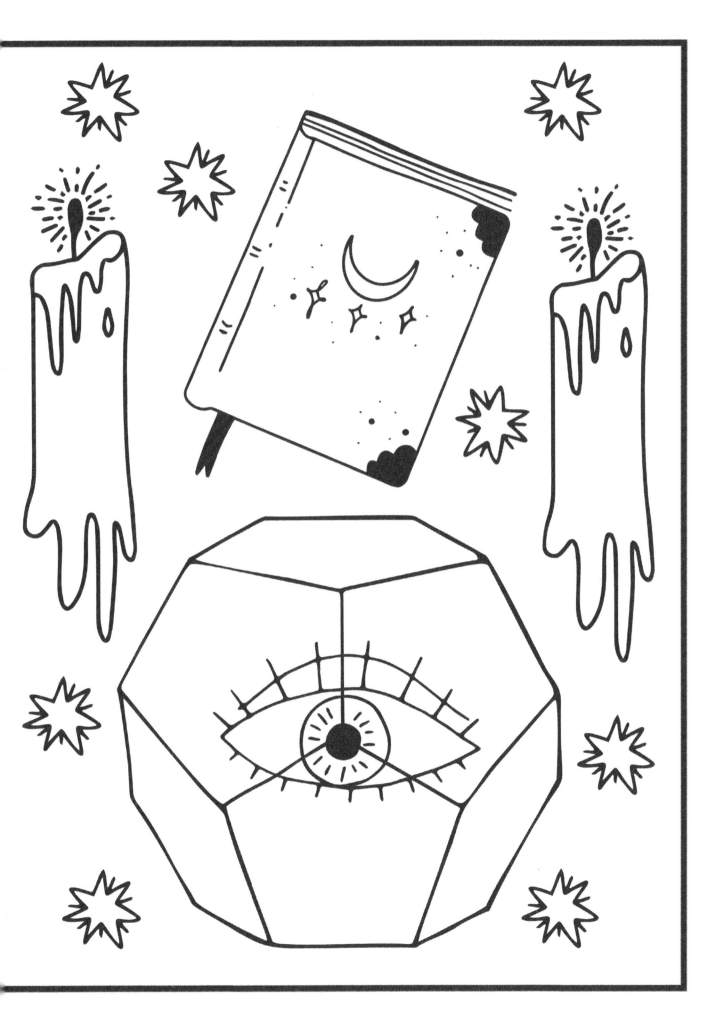

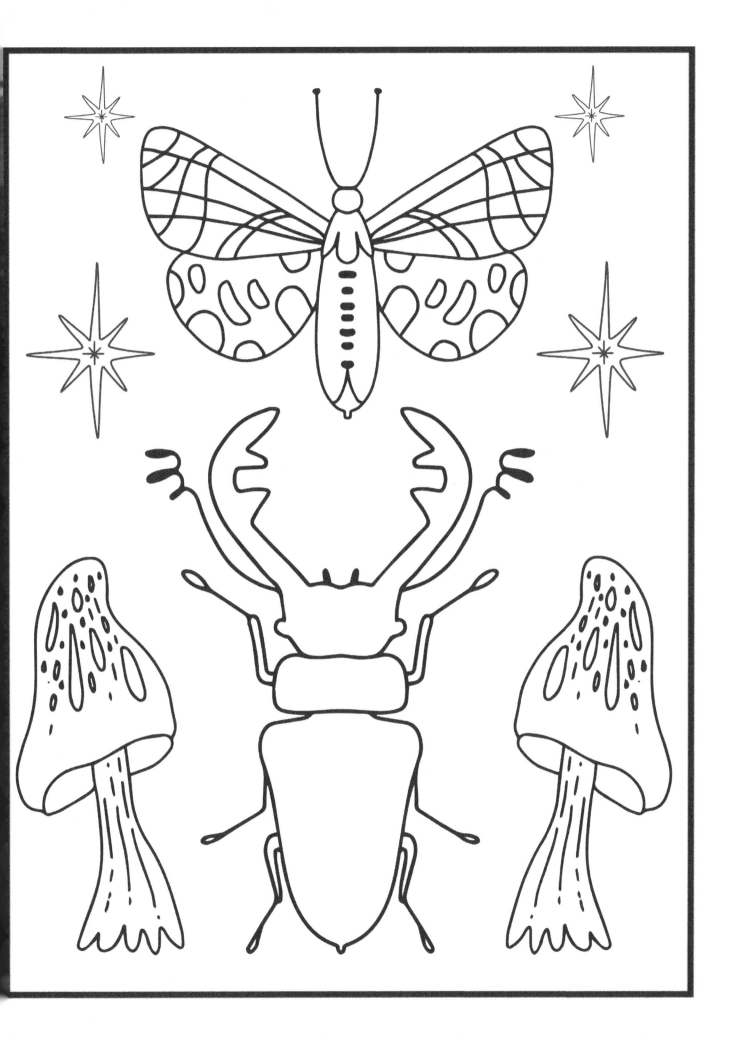

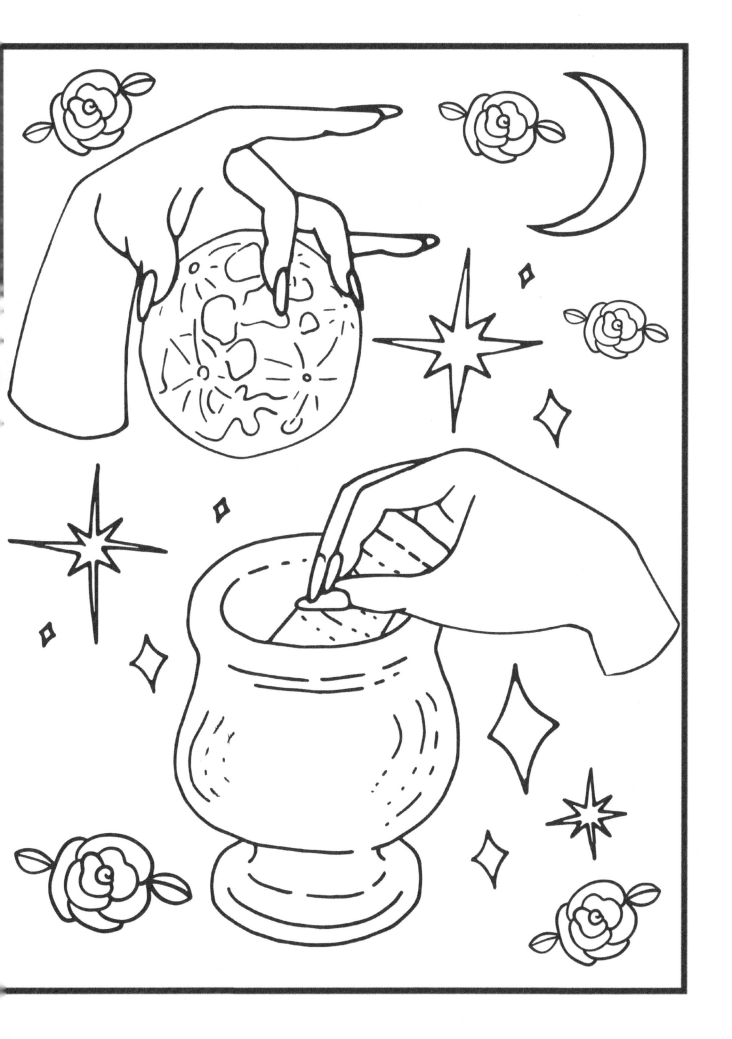

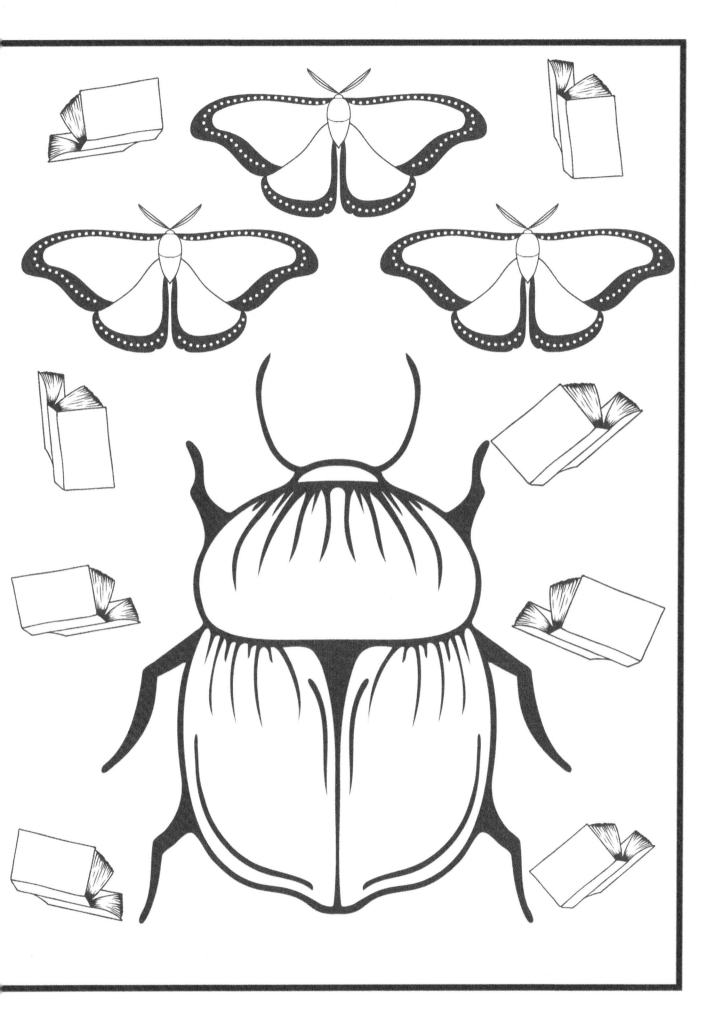

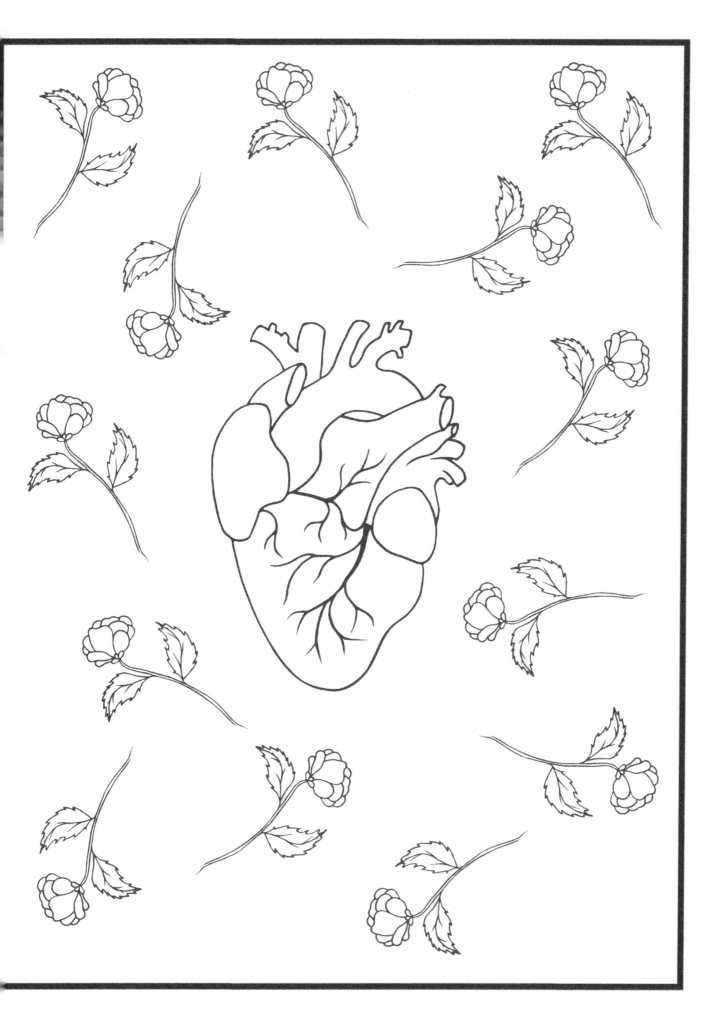

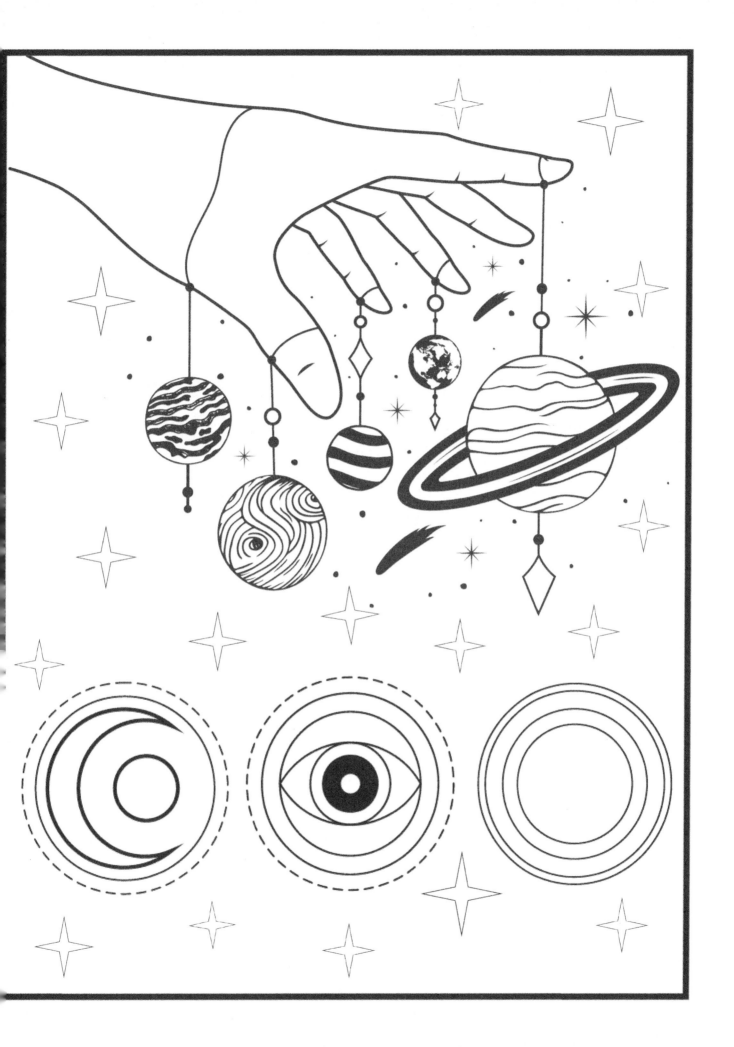

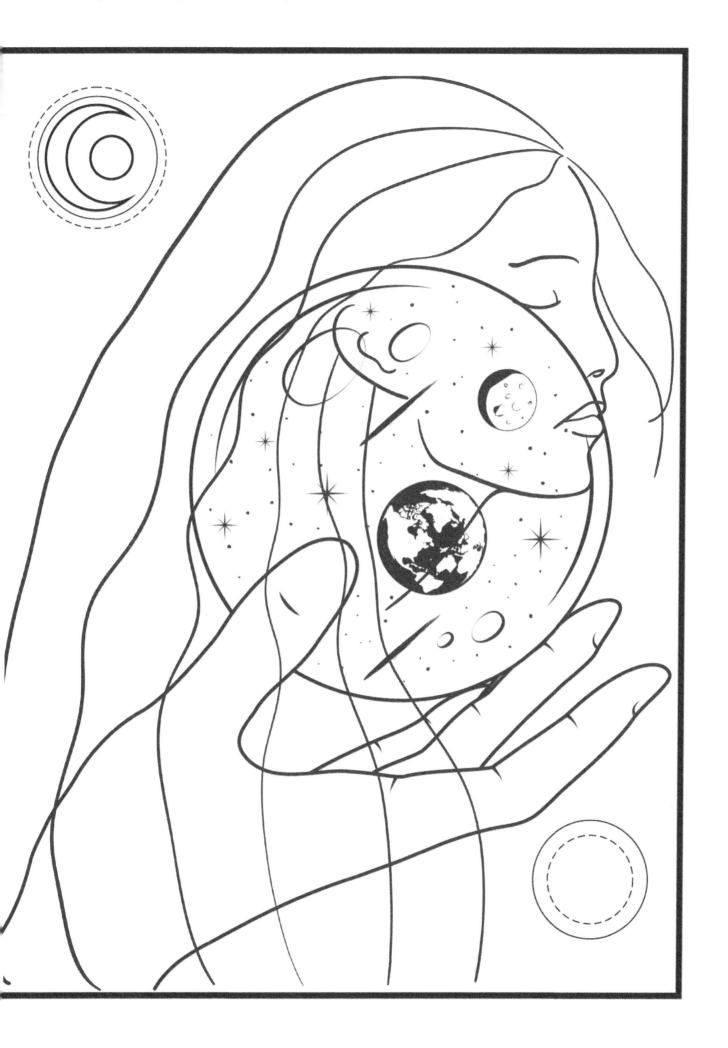

COLOR TEST PAGE

TEST YOUR COLORS HERE & USE AS A REFERENCE GUIDE

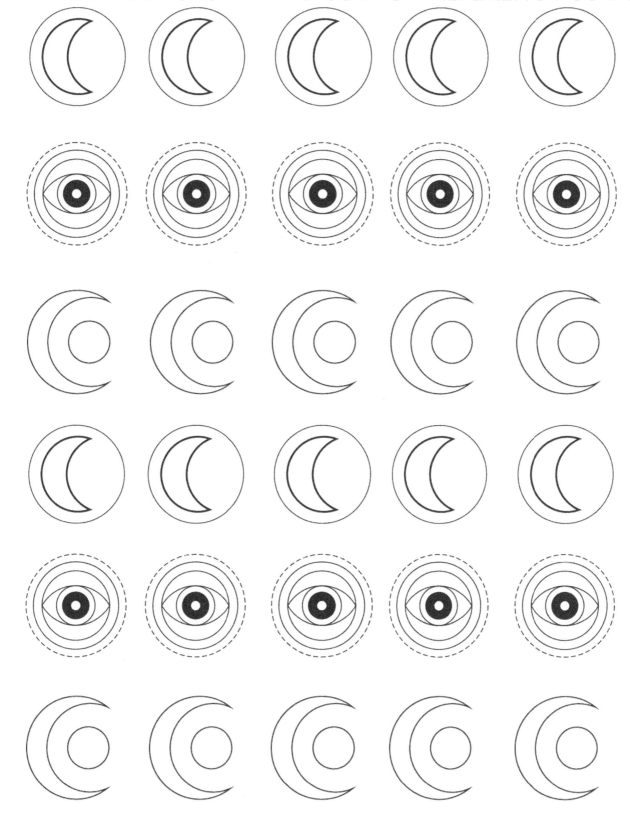

COLOR TEST PAGE

TEST YOUR COLORS HERE & USE AS A REFERENCE GUIDE

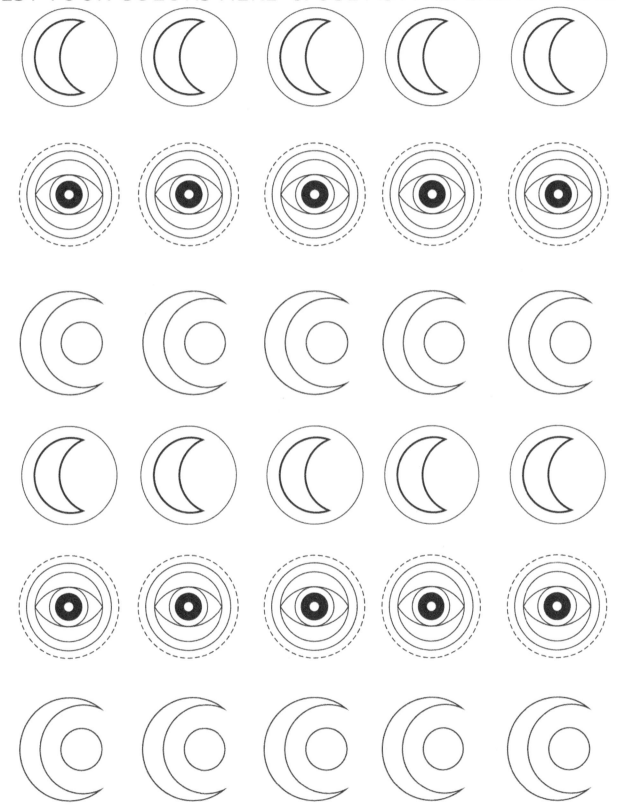

Made in the USA
Monee, IL
31 December 2024

75739319R00059